YOGA
CLASS

HB
HINKLER
BOOKS

Art Director: Karen Moores
Graphic Artist: Post Pre-press Group
Photographer: UB Photo
Editor: Fiona Staun
Special thanks to Alida Hickey

Published in 2004
by Hinkler Books Pty Ltd
17-23 Redwood Drive
Dingley, VIC 3172, Australia
www.hinklerbooks.com

© Hinkler Books Pty Ltd 2004

Printed and bound in China

ISBN 1 7412 1500 5

CONTENTS

INTRODUCTION TO YOGA

Discover your journey to health and harmony

Yoga aims to bring a harmonious balance into our lives. It allows us to let go of the past and future, and to be in the present moment experiencing our true 'Inner Self'. Yoga starts us on the journey towards a healthy and harmonious life.

The word Yoga simply means *Union*. This union implies harmony of mind, body and spirit. It is not associated with any particular religion, or religious group. Yoga has been practiced and passed on for about 5000 years. Originating in India, the first references to yoga, its philosophy and its many postures were discovered in some of the oldest written manuscripts ever found.

YOGA CLASS

Yoga Class is a clear and comprehensive approach to yoga, incorporating some Chi Gung movements. You will find it designed for beginner and intermediate students. *Yoga Class* includes 'natural breathing' – a flowing series of postures and relaxation. It begins with a relaxation period, bringing awareness about our natural breath, followed by a gentle series of limbering up movements to open the joints, unblock and stimulate energy flow. It then moves through a flowing series of dynamic and static postures to cleanse and strengthen, whilst continuing to generate and circulate energy throughout the whole body. The sequence concludes with a meditation to centre the body and mind. Gary Bromley, a true Yoga expert, will gently guide you throughout.

People of all ages and walks of life can enjoy yoga. Don't be concerned if you are unable to perform some of the postures. *Yoga Class* is designed to allow you to work within your own boundaries and remain free from goals. Do not strain or force your body into a posture. With regular practice, your body will become stronger, more flexible, and energy will increase.

So begin your yoga journey with an open mind, allow change to happen and discover the wonderful joy yoga will bring to you.

THE BENEFITS OF YOGA

Yoga helps us to balance our lives, to be happy and healthy and to improve our relationships with our partners, children, friends and ourselves.

YOGA LETS YOU REGAIN CONTROL

As yoga totally embraces our mind, body and spirit, you will find it helps improve relationships, sporting pursuits and our working lives.

Regular practice can help change a negative mindset by offering inner peace and an ability to face upheavals and deal with problems.

AN ABUNDANT LIFE

The benefits of Yoga seem to be endless. It is perfectly adaptable to all kinds of lifestyles – Eastern, Western, children and adults. It can replace the so-called buzzes of alcohol, caffeine, nicotine and other stimulants with a wonderful sense of invigoration. Sports people may find a new sense of energy release. It is a fabulous way to tone and strengthen our bodies.

WELLNESS – NOT ILLNESS

When you regularly practise yoga, you may find it:
- Helps relieve depression and anxiety
- Increases energy levels
- Aids weight control
- Helps relieve arthritis
- Boosts flexibility and energy
- Provides natural stimulation.
- Improves osteoporosis, circulation and digestion and lowers blood pressure

When and Where to Practise Yoga

Yoga is meant to be enjoyable, so it is important to approach your practice with a sense of adventure, purpose and respect.

A Special Place

Find yourself a really special place, as this is your 'time-out'. Make sure it is quiet and peaceful. You need to be comfortable. Rooms should be airy and dust-free. Place your mat towards a door or window. If outside, make sure the conditions are pleasant and face away from the sun, preferably towards a tree or water.

A Special Time

Ideal times for yoga are early morning or early evening.

A Special Way

Yoga is best practised on an empty stomach. In the morning, just have a glass of warm water with lemon on rising. It is best to wait three or four hours after a meal, but some practices can be done after a 'light' meal. A 'bathroom' stop is recommended before you start, too.

A Special Outfit

It is important to wear loose, comfortable clothing when doing yoga. You don't need to buy special clothing, but remember there is lots of sitting, standing and stretching. Take off any jewellery and metal items, and tie the hair back loosely. You also need to stay warm after your session.

What You Need

All you need for the yoga experience is a towel, mat, pillow and a chair – things so easily available.

THE NATURAL BREATH

From the moment of birth, we take our first breath, filling our body with life force. As we continue our life journey, not a minute of the day passes, without us giving nourishment to our body and mind via the breath. Unfortunately, that quality of nourishment can diminish, as we get caught up in the cobweb of life. Our fast pace of life tends to place increasing stress on our bodies, directly and indirectly affecting many physiological processes.

EFFECTS OF STRESS

One of the first reactions to stress in the body is the over-stimulation of our sympathetic nervous system. The diaphragm begins to constrict and sets up rapid shallow breathing. Unbelievably, a vast range of illnesses can occur from this simple reaction. Other factors such as poor posture, diet, muscle tone and emotional responses, can all have an effect on the way we breathe.

BREATH OF LIFE

Being able to breathe correctly will make an enormous difference to your overall health and emotional state. First, breathe in through the nose. Feel the breath below the abdomen. The abdomen will rise on inhalation, then feel the lungs expand like a balloon. When you exhale (through the nose), release your chest and abdomen. Remember not to control or force the breath. Simply observe and feel its rhythmic inhalation and exhalation.

BREATH FOR YOGA

Use your breath as a valuable tool during your Yoga practice. Feel areas of tightness, tension or resistance release with each breath. Experience the flow of energy throughout the body. Avoid trying to force your body deeper into postures which can create further resistance. Learn to use the breath as a tool to create support for your movements, and to release the whole body. Breathing 'naturally' will allow you to experience a more balanced life. It will help you release tension and stress, allow your whole body to function more effectively and clear your mind.

PEACEFUL POSE

SHAVASANA

Relaxes the whole body and mind. Ideally practised before a session to let go of all tension and to bring awareness onto the natural flow of breath below the navel.

1 Lie flat on your back, with legs straight and hip width apart. Allow your legs and feet to roll away from each other, with your arms alongside your body, palms up at a 30–45 degree angle.

2 Gently elongate your neck and tuck your chin in slightly. Close your eyes, feel your posterior body sinking into the floor, and your anterior light and weightless.

3 Bring your awareness onto your natural flow of breath below your navel. Do not try to force or control your breath. Allow your mind to follow the rhythm of your breath and experience the present moment. A state of stillness, peace and inner harmony.

4 Place your right hand below your navel, palm down and left on top. Continue to observe the rising of your abdomen on the inhale and the falling on exhale. Continue for 3–5 minutes before opening your eyes, bending your knees and rolling to your right side coming up to Mountain Pose.

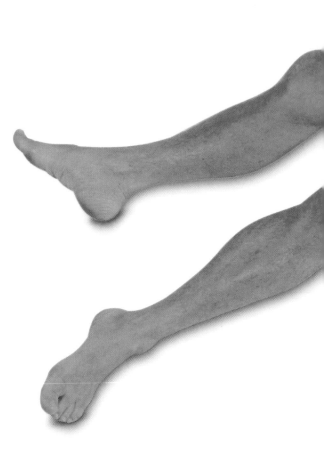

MOUNTAIN POSE

WITH HANDS IN PRAYER POSE

Benefits:
- Bringing your hands into Prayer Pose allows your body/mind to centre
- Harmonises your nervous system
- Energises your heart, pericardium and lungs

1 Stand in Mountain Pose (Page 15) with hands in Prayer Pose. Relax shoulders and lengthen your spine.

2 Close your eyes and continue to observe your natural breath flow. Remain for 30 seconds.

MOUNTAIN POSE

TADASANA

Benefits:
- Tadasana is used as a foundation of all the standing postures and movements
- The natural way to stand – 'a relaxed and steady standing position'
- Cultivates a sense of strength and stability
- Mountain Pose is an effective way of freeing energy that has been blocked by stress and tension
- The primary posture for the absorption of universal energy

1 Begin with your feet between your hips and shoulders – go with what feels natural and comfortable. Slightly angle your feet outwards with your weight evenly spread through the balls, lateral edge and heel. Avoid your arches collapsing inwards. Try to feel them lift up.

2 Unlock your knee joints and tuck your sacrum slightly in. Relax your abdomen and hips.

3 Lengthen up through the spine. Let your arms hang and relax your shoulders.

4 Slightly tuck your chin in, and at the same time, feel the back of your neck lengthen.

5 Soften your eyes, face and relax your jaw. Gaze forward and downward. You should feel as if your head is being suspended from above, at the crown, by an invisible string.

6 Feel energy permeating your body, through the pores of your skin – producing a light, free feeling. Remain for 3 to 5 minutes. Your eyes can remain open or closed.

LIMBERING UP EXERCISES

PAWANMUKTASANA SERIES

1 Begin in Mountain Pose (Page 15). Lower your chin down to your chest and roll your head in a circular pathway to the right. Elongate your neck as it passes the centre position. Repeat 3 times and alternate to the left. Be careful not to bend your neck backwards.

2 Float your arms up to shoulder height, palms down. Swing them behind and out to the side of your body. Repeat 5 times. Roll your shoulders backwards 5 times, alternating shoulders 5 times.

3 Rotate your wrist joint 5 times and alternate. Open and close your hands, stretch through the fingers. Shake your hands to shoulder height and back alongside the body. Relax your face and body.

Benefits:

- Opens your joints and makes your muscles and connective tissue supple
- Stimulates the flow of blood, lymph and cerebrospinal fluid
- Unblocks and stimulates the flow of energy through the meridians
- Warming up helps prepare your body to avoid injury

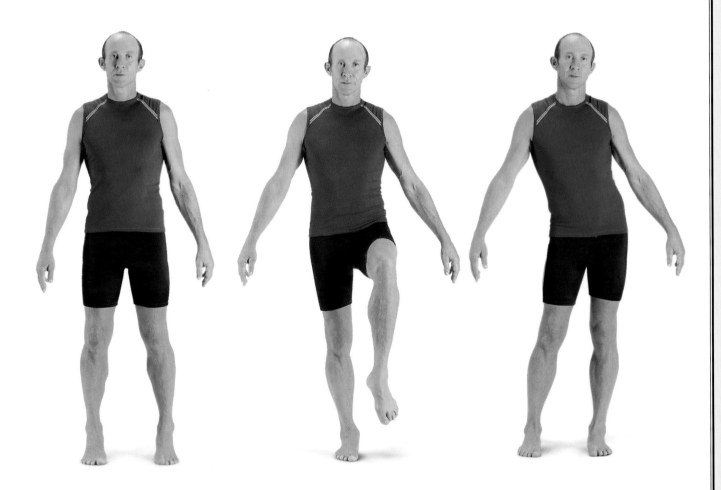

4 Rise onto the balls of your feet, keep your weight even behind the big and little toe. Lower back onto your heels and sink slightly bending your knees. Take care to keep your knees over and behind your toes as you sink. Repeat 5 times.

5 Raise your left leg in front of your body; flex and extend your ankle joint, and then rotate your foot in a circle. Repeat with the right ankle.

6 From Mountain Pose move your hips in a small circle clockwise. Do 5 times clockwise and alternate.

LIMBERING UP EXERCISES

(continued)

7 Using small movements, tuck your pelvis back and under. Keep your upper body stationary. Repeat 5 times. Extend the front of your chest forward, and then lower your chin into your chest. Relax your shoulders. Repeat 5 times.

8 Bend your knees, lower your chin into your chest, relax your shoulders and vertebra-by-vertebra roll down. Keep your knees bent, push through your feet and reverse the downward path back to Mountain Pose. Repeat 3 times.

9 From Mountain Pose, rock forward onto your toes and back onto your heels. Keep the spine lengthened.

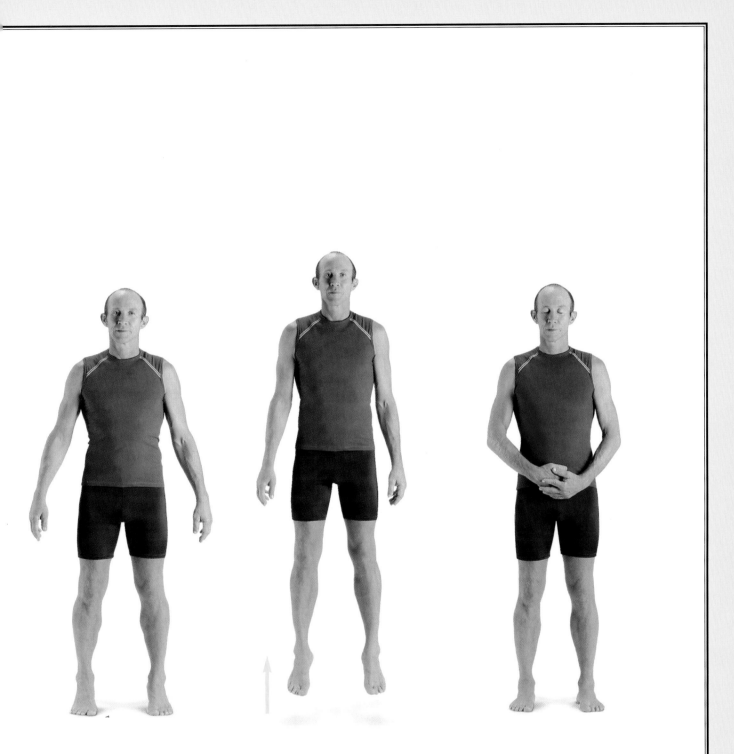

10 Keep your feet grounded and move your body in a bouncing action. Have awareness of fascia releasing. Continue bouncing on the balls of your feet. Keep them grounded, whilst keeping your heels off the ground.

11 From bouncing, continue into small jumps. Keep your ankle and knee joints soft.

SOFTER
Stop at step 10 if you have discomfort.

12 Stand in Mountain Pose, place your right hand below the navel and left hand on top. 'Gather the Chi' and allow your diaphragm to come back to its natural rhythm. Hold for 60 seconds and roll down to Diamond Pose.

DIAMOND POSE

VAJRASANA

Benefits

- Improves flexibility of your spine, ankles, knees, and hips
- Assists digestion and assimilation, both psychological and physiologically
- A meditative pose
- Opens and circulates energy – main central energy channel
- Strengthens and tones your abdomen and spine

STATIC VERSION

1 Kneel on the floor, with your knees and ankles slightly apart. Rest your buttocks on your heels and your palms down on your thighs.

2 Feel your spine and neck lengthening with your chin slightly tucked. Relax your shoulders.

DYNAMIC VERSION

1 Start in Diamond Pose, and then extend your arms overhead bringing your palms together and taking them down through your torso.

2 Rest your palms on your thighs and fold forward from your hips. Keep lengthening through your spine until your lower back releases. Then tuck your chin into your chest and roll up. Repeat 3 to 5 times in a flowing manner.

SOFTER
Place a cushion under your buttocks and calves for a softer feel.

CAT POSE

BIDALASANA

Benefits

- Gentle movement through your spine, shoulders and hips
- Improves blood flow to your spine and spinal nerves
- Strengthens, tones and stretches your abdominal organs and spine
- Improves spinal flexibility
- Opens up your bladder and stomach meridians

DYNAMIC VERSION

1 Start on all fours with knees under hips and hands under shoulders. Make sure your head, neck and spine are parallel to the ground.

2 Take your navel towards the ground and lift your tailbone—feel your sitting bones spread. Avoid taking your head back and continue to lengthen through your crown.

3 Tuck your chin in and round your spine. Feel your navel being drawn up and your buttocks contracting. Repeat, alternating the hollowing and rounding of your spine, five times.

STATIC VERSION

1 Hold Dynamic (step 2) for 10 seconds.

2 Then Dynamic (step 3) for 10 seconds and fold back into Hare Pose. (Page 24)

Avoid any tension while holding the poses.

HARE POSE

SHASHANKASANA

Benefits
- Stretches your lower back
- Relaxes your sciatic nerves
- Strengthens and cleanses your lower lungs and stomach
- Opens the main central energy

1 From Cat Pose (Page 22, step 3) take your buttocks back to your heels. Keep your spine rounded, chin tucked into your chest and keep your hands stationary.

2 Keep your abdomen off your thighs. Hold for 10 seconds.

LIZARD POSE

Utthan Prishasana

Benefits

- Exercises and strengthens your lungs and tones your entire back, especially your nerves and muscles
- Can relieve backache and fatigue
- Cleanses your lungs, liver, spleen and stomach

1 Slide your arms forward from Hare Pose until your thighs remain at right angles to the ground.

2 Rest your forehead on the ground and feel the front of your upper chest release towards the ground.

3 Relax your shoulders and hold for 10 seconds.

CHILD'S POSE

SUPTA VAJRASANA

Benefits
- A relaxation pose that has a calming effect on your nervous system
- Gently opens your hips and entire spine
- Strengthens your kidneys

1 Take your buttocks back to your heels, placing your forehead on the ground. Rest your hands palms down alongside your face.

2 Relax your shoulders and allow your whole body to soften. Hold for 20 seconds.

SOFTER
Place one fist on top of the other and rest your forehead on your two fists for added comfort.

EAGLE FOLDING ITS WINGS

Benefits

- Strengthens and tones your spine, buttocks and abdominal muscles
- Improves flexibility through your spine and back of your legs
- Opens up the flow of energy in all your meridians and vessels
- Increases circulation throughout your body
- Stimulates your endocrine system

1 Begin in Mountain Pose (Page 15). Sink slightly, turn your palms out and raise your arms above your head, rising with the arm movement. Sink as you bring your arms down in front of your torso, palms down. Place the back of your hands in the small of your back. Check that your knees are behind and aligned with your toes.

2 Keeping your head, neck and back vertical, fold forward from the hip joint with a Monkey Back (Page 32, step 2). When your torso is at a right angle to the ground, continue the downward motion by tucking your chin in. Feel your lower back release and roll your shoulders, allowing your arms to come forward under your shoulders palms up.

3 With the knees bent and weight evenly under your feet, keep your chin tucked in and roll up to Mountain Pose. Repeat 3 times.

SOFTER

If you experience pain or tightness at step 2 leave your arms to the side, tuck your chin in and roll down. Continue step 3.

TORTOISE SERIES

Benefits

- Strengthens and tones your spine, abdomen and legs
- Stretches your spine and back of your legs
- Circulates blood and energy around your body
- Strengthens your kidneys, lungs and heart
- Opens your kidney, liver, spleen and bladder meridians

1 Begin in Mountain Pose and turn your left foot out approximately half a hip width. Turn your feet to be on a 30 to 45 degree angle. Sink down slightly, bending your knees and keeping your weight evenly distributed under your feet. Place the back of your hands in the small of your back.

2 Keeping your body vertical, fold from your hip joint until at a right angle to the ground (The Tortoise). Look to the ground between your legs and feel your spine lengthen. Keep the natural lumber curve in your spine and check your knees are behind and aligned with your toes. Hold for 10 seconds.

3 Tucking your chin into your chest, fold forwards rolling your shoulders and bringing your hands (palms up) to relax on the ground. Keep your knees bent and feel the stretch through your spine (Tortoise Forward Bend). Hold for 10 to 20 seconds.

4 From the Tortoise Forward Bend, slowly sink your buttocks towards the ground to an approximate 45 degree angle and return to the starting position. Repeat 5 times slowly and hold the fifth squat (Tortoise Squat). Check your knee-toe alignment. Hold for 5 seconds.

5 From the Tortoise Squat, return to a Tortoise Forward Bend and lengthen through your legs and spine. Keep your knee joints unlocked. Hold for 10 to 20 seconds and roll back up to starting position.

SOFTER

If your hips and spine are tight, leave out step 2 and roll down, continue step 3. Another option until your spine and hips gain strength and suppleness is to use a chair. If step 4 creates strain leave it out of your practice, until you are ready.

CAUTION

If you suffer from any condition where your head should not be below the level of your heart, bend half way only.

MONKEY SERIES

Benefits
- Has all the benefits of the Tortoise series (Page 30)
- Gives a gentle massage to your liver and spleen, and aids digestion
- Has a calming influence on your nervous system.
- Helps with anxiety and depression

1 Begin in Mountain Pose, sink down slightly, bending your knees and keeping your weight evenly distributed under your feet. Place your hands in the small of your back.

2 Keep your spine vertical and fold forward from your hips. When your torso is at a right angle to the ground, hold statically (The Monkey). Check your knees are over and behind your toes. Hold for 10 seconds.

3 Release your lower back, tuck your chin in and roll forward. Place your hands (palms up) on the ground (Monkey Forward Bend). Keeping your torso centered between your legs, extend through the back of your legs. Check your knee joints are soft and unlocked. Hold for 10 seconds.

4 Bend your knees a little more and concentrate on stretching your sacrum and lower back. Hold for 10 seconds.

5 Maintaining the stretch on your lower back, slowly begin to lengthen the backs of your legs. You should feel an equal stretch on both. Hold for 10 seconds.

6 From Monkey Forward Bend, slowly lower your buttocks 90⁰ to the ground, and in a continuous movement, rise back to starting position. Repeat 5 times and hold the fifth squat for 5 seconds. Check your knee alignment and keep your weight even under your feet.

7 From the Monkey Squat, place your hands around the outside of your ankles and lengthen through the back of the legs, into a Monkey Forward Bend. Relax your neck and shoulders and feel the crown of your head release towards the ground. Keep your knee joints unlocked. Hold for 10 seconds. Bend your knees, repeat step 4 and roll back up to Mountain Pose.

Palm Tree

Benefits
- Counter posture for forward bends
- Lengthens your spine
- Strengthens your upper body
- Promotes better body alignment and the even muscle development on both sides of your body
- Opens and strengthens your heart and lungs

1 Roll up from Monkey Forward Bend – raise your arms overhead with your elbows bent and palms facing inwards.

2 Keep your sacrum slightly tucked and feel the lengthening through your spine.

DOWNWARD DOG

ADHO MUKHA SVANANA

Benefits

- Stretches your Achilles' tendons, hamstring and calf muscles. Tones your sciatic nerve
- Strengthens your upper body. Stretches and relaxes your spine
- Improves your circulation to your brain
- Opens your bladder, gallbladder, heart and lung meridian

SOFTER

If you have tight hamstrings or hip flexors, keep your knees very bent.

CAUTION

Avoid if you have high blood pressure or a heart condition.

1 Roll down onto all fours. Tuck your toes under and push back with your hands while raising your hips up and back.

2 Press your heels towards the ground, keeping your knees slightly bent. Aim to distribute your weight evenly between hands and feet, so that your body forms an inverted 'V'.

3 Relax your neck muscles and roll your shoulders inwards, spreading your shoulder blades. Hold for 10 seconds.

THE CRESCENT MOON

CHANDRASANA

Benefits

- Stretches and opens your hips and helps relieve sciatica
- Increases the circulation to your pelvic area
- Strengthens your digestive system, heart, liver and lungs
- Helps improve concentration and balance to the nervous system

1 From Downward Dog, kneel on all fours or in a flowing action, bring your left leg forward. Point your toes on the right foot behind you. Your left knee is placed directly over your heel, feel the front of your right hip release. Your hands and fingers are placed on either side of your left foot, with fingers pointing forward.

2 When you are stable, bring your torso into an upright position and place your left hand on your thigh, right hand on top. Keep your pelvis stable and lengthen up through the spine. Eyes looking forward. Hold for 10 seconds.

3 Keep lifting your chest up as you extend your arms up, lengthening from your shoulders. Relax your shoulders away from the ears and keep the stretch through your spine. Hold for 10 seconds.

4 Bring your arms down and place your hands under your shoulders (fingers forward). Move your left leg back and come into Downward Dog (Page 35). Hold for 5 seconds and repeat steps 1 to 4 using your right leg.

VINE POSE

GARUDASANA

Benefits
- Stretches your ankles, knees and hips
- Strengthens and opens your thoracic spine
- Cleanses your lungs, heart, liver and stomach
- Opens the triple heater and small intestine meridians

1 Come into Diamond Pose (Page 20). Raise your arms to shoulder height and bring your right arm across your left above the elbow. Bend your elbow and twist your right arm around your left arm until your palms can be placed together. Your thumbs should point towards your nose.

2 Focus on lengthening through your spine and relaxing your shoulders.

DIAMOND POSE
WITH SHOULDER EXTENSION

Benefits

- Stretches tight ankles and quadriceps. Opens your chest and releases tension in tight shoulders.
- Stretches muscles involved in respiration for better breathing
- Strengthens your heart and lungs.
- Opens your heart, lungs and pericardium meridan

1 Sit in Diamond Pose (Page 20), extend your arms overhead and interlace your fingers as you turn the palms upward. Keep your gaze forward.

2 Relax your shoulders and continue to lengthen your spine upwards.

SOFTER
If you have tightness in your joints, place a cushion under your buttocks.

TIGER POSE

VYAGHRASANA

Benefits
- Improves spinal flexibility, relaxes your sciatic nerves
- Tones your abdomen, hips and thighs
- Strengthens your nervous system and activates circulation to all the organs
- Cleanses your colon and lungs
- Opens your bladder meridan

DYNAMIC VERSION

1 Begin on all fours. Extend your right leg back, parallel to the ground. Check your pelvis is stable, bend your right knee and point your toes towards the back of your head. Look downward.

2 Swing the bent leg under your right hip and take your knee toward your chest. Tuck your chin into your chest. Keep your ankle, knee and hip alignment. Continue dynamically 5 times and repeat left side.

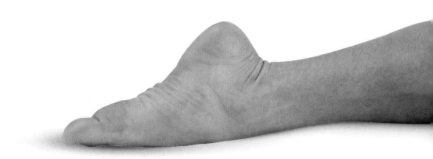

STAFF POSE

DANDASANA

Benefits
- Stretches and extends your spine
- Effective for toning your whole body and helps develop postural strength
- Strengthens your heart and lungs
- Opens your stomach meridian

1 Begin seated, extending to straight legs keeping your knee joints unlocked, feet are hip width apart, toes pointing upwards.

2 Place your hands behind you, palms down, fingers spread, and relax your shoulders.

3 Balance on your sitting bones and lengthen through your spine. Lift your chest and open your heart centre. Hold for 20 seconds. To increase the effectiveness of this pose, keep your spine vertical and retain its natural curve.

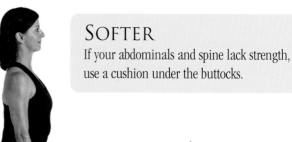

SOFTER
If your abdominals and spine lack strength, use a cushion under the buttocks.

SITTING FORWARD BEND

PASCIMOTTANASANA

Benefits

- Opens and elongates all the muscles of your back, particularly in the sacral area
- Stretches your hamstrings and loosens your hips
- Calms your nervous system
- Strengthens your kidneys and cleanses your digestive system, liver and spleen
- Opens your bladder meridan

1 From Staff Pose (Page 44) raise your arms above your head, elbows bent palms forward. Keep the length through your spine.

SITTING
FORWARD BEND

(continued)

2 Anchor your buttocks and fold forward from your hip joints. Without rounding your spine, rest your hands alongside your shins, ankles or feet.

3 If you have the flexibility, continue to fold forward and rest your head between your shins. Hold for 20 seconds.

4 Return to an upright position by reversing the path taken into the forward bend.

SOFTER

If your lower back rounds, sit on a cushion so that your hips are raised slightly. Hold a towel around your feet and keep your spine lengthening up and forward.

SITTING HALF TWIST

ARDA MATSYENDRASANA

Benefits
- Tones your spinal nerves, makes your back muscles supple and loosens your vertebrae
- Cleanses and massages your digestive system, liver, pancreas, kidneys and spleen
- Opens your gallbladder meridian

1 Sit with your legs crossed and with your back upright. Place your right hand out to the side of your buttocks and come onto your fingertips. Your left hand rests on the outside of your right knee.

2 Extend up through your spine and head. Stabilise your pelvis and twist to the right commencing from the lumber spine and continuing up. Keep your shoulders level throughout.

3 Continue to lengthen your spine. Hold for 10 seconds and repeat opposite side

SOFTER
If your back is not straight, sit on a cushion throughout so that your hips are raised slightly.

CROCODILE TWIST

JATHARA PARIVARTANASANA

Benefits
- Stretches your lower back and sciatic nerves. Relieves backache
- Aligns your spinal vertebrae
- Cleanses your digestive system, liver and gallbladder
- Opens your gallbladder meridian

1 Lie on your back with your arms outstretched at shoulder height, palms up. Bend your knees and place your soles on the ground a little wider than hip width apart. Relax your abdomen.

DYNAMIC VERSION

2 Lower your knees to the right and look towards your left shoulder. Keep both feet and shoulders in contact with the ground. Bring your knees back to centre then alternate to the left, and look towards your right hand. Continue dynamically for 45 seconds.

STATIC VERSION

3 Hold the twist for 10 seconds each side and return your legs to centre.

KNEE TO CHEST POSE

Benefits
- Opens your hips
- Stretches your lower back and sciatic nerves
- Massages your abdominal organs
- Opens your bladder meridian

1 Lying on your back, bring your right leg up. Interlace your fingers below your knee and take your knee to chest.

2 Keep your chin tucked and spine extended. Hold for 10 seconds, and continue into Lever Pose (Page 51, steps 1–3). Repeat with your left leg.

LEVER POSE

Benefits

- Helps relieve backache
- Opens your lower thoracic and lumber spine
- Gives a gentle squeeze to your abdominal organs and helps peristalsis in your intestines
- Increases a sense of vitality
- Opens your bladder and gallbladder meridian

1 Place your left hand on the outside of your right knee. Extend your right arm out from your shoulder (palms up).

2 Relax your abdomen and lower your right knee to the left. Look at your right hand. Hold for 10 seconds.

3 Return your leg to the centre and extend out straight.

4 Repeat with your left leg, Knee to Chest Pose (Page 50) then above steps 1–3.

5 Come into Womb Pose (Page 54) as a counter pose.

HALF BRIDGE

SETU BANKHA SARVANANGASANA

Benefits
- Stretches and massages your colon and other abdominal organs
- Stretches the front of your hips, increasing flexibility
- Nourishes your thyroid gland with a fresh blood supply
- Strengthens your lungs, heart, liver, spleen, stomach and cleanses your kidneys and spine
- Opens your stomach meridian

1 Lie on your back. Bring your feet up towards your buttocks as far as they will comfortably go. Place your feet hip width apart. Place your arms at your side, palms down. Lengthen through your spine and keep your chin slightly tucked in.

DYNAMIC VERSION

2 Begin by pressing down on the floor with your feet and slowly raise your hips. Feel one vertebra at a time peeling off the floor. The weight of your body is equally supported by your feet, shoulders, and arms. Keep your chest lifting and opening, and legs parallel.

3 Return to lying on your back by reversing the motion. Move very slowly replacing vertebra by vertebra onto the ground. Rest with the back of your abdomen flat on the ground. Repeat 3 times holding the third bridge statically.

STATIC VERSION

4 Hold the bridge keeping your feet and shoulders stationary. Keep your shoulders relaxed and chin tucked in. Hold for 10 seconds and return to starting position.

CAUTION

Avoid during pregnancy, if you have high blood pressure or a heart condition.

WOMB POSE

ASPANASANA

Benefits

- Stretches your lower back and hips
- Stretches your sciatic nerves
- Excellent for digestion, massaging your large and small intestine
- Counter posture to backbends, twist and strong standing postures

1 Lie on your back, bend one leg up at a time, holding below your knee take your thighs into your abdomen. Keep your knees hip width apart and relax your neck and shoulders. Elongate through the back of your neck, keeping your chin tucked in. Hold for 20 seconds.

2 Return to starting position by extending out one leg at a time.

BIRTH POSE

Benefits

- Stretches your groin and hips
- Increases circulation to your pelvic cavity
- Strengthens your kidneys, uterus and genitals
- Opens your kidney, liver and spleen meridians

1 Lie on your back and bring your feet towards your buttocks until comfortable. Place your arms at your side, palms up. Join the soles together and slowly allow your knees to fall outwards, towards the earth. Allow the natural arch to remain in the spine. Close your eyes and observe the rhythmic flow of breath below your navel. Hold for 60 seconds.

PEACEFUL POSE

SHAVASANA

Benefits

- Relaxes your whole body and mind
- A counter posture to all the previous Asanas
- Allows you to fully absorb the energy that has been released and accumulated throughout the *Yoga Class*
- During relaxation your body can recuperate, repair and rejuvenate itself
- An opportunity to surrender any resistance, let go and 'be at peace'

1 Repeat steps 1 to 3 (Page 12). Remain in Peaceful Pose for 5 minutes or longer.

2 Bring your awareness back to your body giving your toes and fingers a wriggle. Keeping your eyes closed bend your right leg, then left. Roll to your right side and come up to sitting cross-legged.

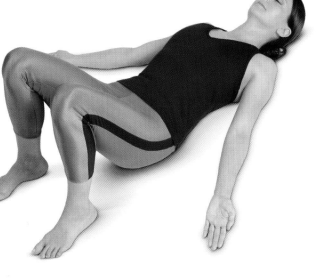

SOFTER
If you have lower back pain, bend your knees and rest the soles of your feet hip width apart. Remain comfortable.

PRAYER POSE
SITTING CROSS LEGGED WITH HANDS IN PRAYER POSE

DHYANA

Benefits
- A concluding posture to allow your energy to settle
- Integrates your thinking and feeling centres

1 Sit cross-legged with your eyes closed. Lengthen your spine.

2 Bring your hands into Prayer Pose. Be with your breath below the navel for a few moments. Feel a sense of calmness and joy wash down through your body. Slowly open your eyes.

'NAMASTE'

Let Food Be Your Medicine

To gain the most out of Yoga, certain awareness must also be placed on what we put into our bodies. Unfortunately over the years our Western dietary choices have placed most peoples' health on 'Red Alert'. From an early age, we are brought up on a diet of commercially packaged, de-vitalized and nutrient-deficient foods. This leaves our bodies depleted of vitamins and minerals, and vulnerable to many illnesses. Fortunately, through the right dietary choices, we can begin to provide our bodies with the nutrients it requires for better health and longevity. This will also benefit our bodies and mind to become more balanced, throughout your yoga practice.

Traditional medicine is based on the premise that there is a self regulating, self healing power within each person, and when the correct nutrients and conditions are provided, the human body is able to heal itself.

A healthy diet is one which is enjoyable and nutritious. The primary reason for eating food is to nourish the body and produce life energy (Chi). It is abundant in whole 'natural' and unprocessed foods. It is especially high in plant foods, such as fruits, vegetables, grains, beans, seeds and nuts.

Food as Medicine

Plants absorb minerals from the soil and water. Through the action of photosynthesis they manufacture vitamins, fatty acids, carbohydrates and proteins. Unfortunately, at times, even if we are complying with a healthy diet, our body is not getting its nutritional requirements met. This may be attributed to poor digestion and assimilation, mineral deficient soils, monocrop farming, use of insecticides and herbicides, air and water pollution. The way food is transported, stored and processed also diminishes it nutrient value, especially its vitamin content.

To ensure your body is receiving optimum health and nutritional requirements, 'Super Foods' – high in natural vitamins, minerals, essential fatty acids, proteins, enzymes and antioxidants – should be considered.

Superfoods

- **Spirulina, Wheat grass, Green Barley Powder**
  Contains 98 out of 100 earth elements. Rich in chlorophyll, which bears a close resemblance to haemoglobin.

- **Vegetable Juice**
  Carrot, beetroot, celery and ginger. A wonderful elixir to cleanse the body. Contains a wide spectrum of vitamins, enzymes and alkalizing minerals.

- **Fatty Acids**
  Equal portions of olive and linseed with a small portion of wheat germ oil. Gives the body its requirements of Omega 3 and Omega 6 essential fatty acids.

- **Seaweed/Kelp Powder**
  One of the most nutritious foods on the earth. High in minerals, especially trace minerals, vitamin B12.

- **Pollen Granules**
  A rich natural source of amino acids. Recognized as a complete food.

- **Royal Maca**
  A natural phytoestrogen. Rich in minerals and trace minerals.

- **Rosehip Powder**
  High in natural Vitamin C and minerals.

DIGESTION ROUTINE

To improve digestion, the following postures can be practised after a meal. Begin with:
• Peaceful Pose (Page 12)
• The Main Central Energy Series (Page 20–27)
• Crocodile Twist (Page 48)
• Womb Pose (Page 54)
• Peaceful Pose (Page 12)

Certain kinds of foods may also influence the body and mind in ways that are either beneficial or detrimental to health. This may depend on the individuals Ayurvedic type or blood type. The importance of correct food-combining of major food groups, such as proteins and carbohydrates, fruit and vegetables also needs to be addressed. For more specific personal advice contact your closest Ayurvedic Naturopath or Health Care Practitioner.

GLOSSARY

ASANA
A yoga posture, a combination of physical alignment and mental awareness

AYURVEDA
Traditional healing system of India. It is a complete health system for mind, body and spirit. Works holistically to prevent and treat disease.

CEREBROSPINAL FLUID
Plasma-like fluid that fills the cavities of the central nervous system.

CERVICAL
The neck.

CHI
Life force, energy.

CHI GUNG
A collective term for various arts that develop energy for health, martial arts, mental training and spiritual development.

CHLOROPHYLL
The green pigment of plants that traps the energy of sunlight.

CONNECTIVE TISSUE
A primary tissue. Functions include support, storage and protection.

DIAPHRAGM
Dome-shaped skeletal muscle between the thoracic and abdominal cavities.

DYNAMIC VERSION
A continuous movement throughout a posture. Circulates energy.

ENDOCRINE SYSTEM
Body system that includes internal organs that secrete hormones.

FASCIA
Layers of fibrous tissue covering and separating muscles.

HATHA
Refers to the balance of male and female. When applied, brings the two sides of the body into balance.

HAEMOGLOBIN
A substance in red blood cells, involved in the transport of oxygen and carbon dioxide.

LATERAL
Relating to the side or sides.

LUMBAR SPINE
Portion of the back between the thorax and the pelvis.

MAIN CENTRAL ENERGY
A circular flow of energy commencing from the base, up the back, and down the front of the body. It is made up of the governing (yang) and conception (ying) vessels.

MERIDIANS
Pathways of energy flow in the body.

PHYTOESTROGEN
A plant molecule that regulates the body's natural estrogen.

PRANA
Life force, life energy.

SACRUM
The large wedge shape bone in the lower part of the back.

SCIATIC NERVES
Two nerves that descend from the lower back through the thigh down the back of the legs.

STATIC VERSION
Holding a posture. Directs energy.

SYMPATHETIC NERVOUS SYSTEM
Primarily concerned with the processes involving the expenditure of energy, i.e. 'fight' or 'flight' response.

THORACIC
The part of the body enclosed by the ribs.

VESSELS
Pathways of energy flow in the body.

ABOUT THE AUTHOR

GARY BROMLEY

Gary Bromley is a highly experienced practitioner in the field of Natural Therapies.

He is involved in the study and practice of Yoga, Chi Gung, Naturopathy and Ayurvedic Medicine – a traditional healing system.

A passionate believer in 'Preventative Medicine', Gary has created his own totally natural health-care range using only 100% natural ingredients.

A special understanding of natural medicine and it's health benefits, has enabled Gary to provide a health care program tailored specifically to suit each individual, which in turn attracts clients to his health clinic on the Gold Coast in Queensland, Australia.

He will offer you a warm welcome, and be happy to answer your questions about *Yoga Class*.